Jeff Bezos
and Amazon

Other titles in the *Technology Titans* series include:

Elon Musk and Tesla

Larry Page, Sergey Brin, and Google

Mark Zuckerberg and Facebook

Reed Hastings and Netflix

Steve Jobs and Apple

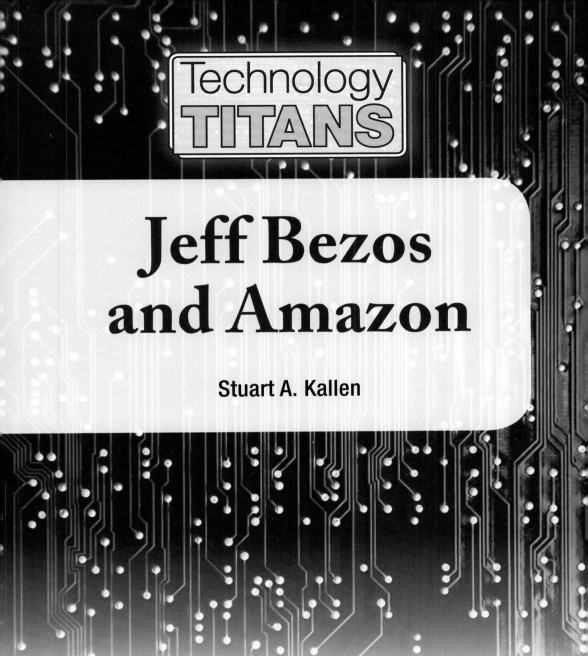

Technology
TITANS

Jeff Bezos and Amazon

Stuart A. Kallen

ReferencePoint
Press®

San Diego, CA

© 2016 ReferencePoint Press, Inc.
Printed in the United States

For more information, contact:
ReferencePoint Press, Inc.
PO Box 27779
San Diego, CA 92198
www.ReferencePointPress.com

LIBRARY OF CONGRESS CATALOGING-IN-PUBLICATION DATA

Kallen, Stuart A., 1955-
  Jeff Bezos and Amazon / by Stuart A. Kallen.
     pages cm. -- (Technology titans)
  Includes bibliographical references and index.
  ISBN-13: 978-1-60152-872-8 (hardback)
  ISBN-10: 1-60152-872-8 (hardback)
  1. Bezos, Jeffrey--Juvenile literature. 2. Amazon.com (Firm)--History--Juvenile literature.
  3. Booksellers and bookselling--United States--Biography--Juvenile literature. 4. Businessmen--United States--Biography--Juvenile literature. 5. Internet bookstores--United States--History--Juvenile literature. 6. Electronic commerce--United States--History--Juvenile literature. I. Title.
  Z473.B47K35 2016
  381.45002092--dc23
  [B]
                                                    2015010389

Contents

A Better Way of Doing Things

In 1988 Jeff Bezos was a twenty-four-year-old information specialist at a New York financial institution called Bankers Trust. Few people knew about the Internet, which would not be accessible to the public until 1989. But Bezos had a vision of the future that exceeded what many thought was possible. He created a digital network that allowed Bankers Trust customers to keep track of their investments on their home computers. This was an untested idea at the time, and Bezos worked hard to convince his boss, Harvey Hirsch, to set up the network. It was an immediate hit with customers, which led Hirsch to say that Bezos "sees a different way of doing things and better ways of doing things."[1]

Bezos's different way of doing things can be traced back to his childhood in Houston, Texas. He was a young inventor who tinkered in the garage and created numerous electronic contraptions. When the first Apple computers appeared in stores in 1977, Bezos was only thirteen, but he learned how to write programs for the machine. And while in high school in Miami, Bezos made plans to build permanent colonies in orbiting space stations.

The Largest in the World

Today Bezos is best known as the founder and CEO of Amazon, the largest and most successful Internet-based retailer in the United States. With a personal net worth of more than $32 billion, Bezos is the seventeenth-richest person in the world. Thanks to Amazon, people today can buy almost anything online. But when Bezos started the company in 1994, he took a huge risk to pursue his dream. He was earning a large salary, and the World Wide Web was still in its infancy. No one had started an online retail company, and it was not clear that people would be interested in shopping from a computer screen.

Although success was hardly guaranteed, Bezos picked a name for his company that fit his ambitions. After searching the dictionary, he picked the name of the Amazon River in South America. *Amazon* sounded different and exotic, and the river was the largest in the world by volume. Bezos hoped the words *different*, *exotic*, and *largest in the world* would someday apply to his online store.

The Amazon website went live on July 16, 1995, and the site initially sold only books. Within a year the company had 150 employees. By 1997 Bezos and his family members who had invested in Amazon were multi-millionaires. By the early 2000s Amazon was offering an array of products that included music, movies, electronics, toys, jewelry, clothing, and nearly anything else a consumer could want. In 2014 Amazon operated in forty-five countries and offered an estimated 200 million products in thirty-five different categories.

> "To me Amazon is a story of a brilliant founder who personally drove the vision."[2]
>
> —Eric Schmidt, chair of Google.

"A Brilliant Founder"

Eric Schmidt, chair of Google, said this about Bezos: "To me Amazon is a story of a brilliant founder who personally drove the vision. There are almost no better examples. . . . Jeff was very garrulous [talkative], very smart. He's a classical technical founder of a business, who understands every detail and cares about it more than anyone."[2]

Driven by Bezos's vision, Amazon has expanded into other markets. Today it creates its own television series, streams video and music, and produces high-tech digital devices such as the Kindle e-book reader and the Kindle Fire tablet computer. Bezos even took a step back into the old media world, purchasing the *Washington Post* newspaper for $250 million in 2013. Looking to the future, Bezos is conducting extensive research to deliver Amazon products by drone. And he founded an aerospace company called Blue Origin with plans to take tourists into outer space.

Those who work with Bezos say he can be a terrifying boss who yells at employees. His business practices have also been blamed for destroying Amazon's competitors. Those who support Bezos say he is driven to provide his customers with the best experience possible. If feelings get hurt or other companies cannot compete, that is simply part of the competitive retail game.

Perhaps Bezos's personal philosophy is best summed up by a pithy thought from the commencement speech he gave at Princeton University in 2010: "When you are eighty years old, and in a quiet moment of

Jeff Bezos took a huge risk when he opened an online bookstore. However, his perseverance and customer-focused business practices have helped Amazon succeed and have made him one of the wealthiest individuals in the world.

reflection narrating for only yourself, the most personal version of your life story . . . will be the series of choices you have made. In the end, we are our choices."[3]

With the founding of Amazon, Bezos made a choice that changed the world. From China to Germany to the United States, a click of the mouse has replaced traveling to the retail store to shop. Although Amazon is no longer exotic or different, it remains, like the river, the largest in the world. And with Bezos at the helm, it is likely that new ideas will just keep flowing into the future.

"Your life story . . . will be the series of choices you have made. In the end, we are our choices."[3]

—Jeff Bezos, founder of Amazon.

Chapter 1

Resourceful and Intelligent

In the mid-1970s an advertising executive named Julie Ray enrolled her son in the Vanguard Gifted and Talented student program at River Oaks Elementary School in Houston, Texas. Ray was captivated by the bright, creative kids she met at River Oaks and decided to write a book about the Vanguard program. While conducting research, Ray met a talkative sixth-grader named Jeff. He was a voracious reader who was working to obtain a reward certificate for reading thirty books during the school year. Ray noted in her book that Jeff was very competitive and focused on winning.

Being the number one reader in River Oaks was only one of Jeff's projects. He told Ray that in math class he had developed a method to evaluate the performance of the school's sixth-grade teachers. Jeff had students fill out surveys on their teachers, which he used to produce charts and graphs on teacher effectiveness. Jeff also excelled in science. While in sixth grade he entered three projects in a local science contest in which most other contestants were in junior or senior high school. Ray recalled years later what one of Jeff's teachers had said about him: "There is probably no limit to what he can do."[4]

The teacher was right about her student, now known to the world as Jeff Bezos (pronounced *Bay-zose*). As the founder and CEO of Amazon, Bezos never seemed to place limits on what he could accomplish.

Family Gumption

Jeffrey Preston Bezos was born on January 12, 1964, in Albuquerque, New Mexico. His mother, Jacklyn (Jackie) Gise Jorgensen, was only seventeen when Jeff was born. Jeff never knew his father, Ted Jorgensen. He abandoned the family when Jeff was only eighteen months old.

Jeff considers Mike Bezos to be his father. Mike was a Cuban refugee who came to the United States alone in 1962 at age fifteen. Mike ended up living in a Catholic mission in Delaware with fifteen other refugees. He learned English, graduated high school, and moved to New Mexico to attend the University of Albuquerque (now called the University of New Mexico). Mike had a part-time job in a bank, where he met Jackie. The two were married in 1968. Mike soon earned an engineering degree and moved the family to Houston, where he began a thirty-year career as a petroleum engineer with Exxon. Mike adopted Jeff and had two children with Jackie: Christina, born in 1969, and Mark, born in 1970.

As an adult, Jeff Bezos refused to discuss his biological father, saying he never met the man. According to reporter Michael Granberry, Bezos "credits much of his gumption and sense of survival to [Mike Bezos] the only man he'll ever call 'Dad.'"[5]

"A Towering Figure"

Bezos's other major influence was his maternal grandfather, Lawrence Preston Gise. As far as Bezos was concerned, Gise had held some of the coolest jobs in the world. In the 1950s Gise was a real rocket scientist who worked on space and missile technology for the US Department of Defense. In the 1960s Gise was appointed by Congress to oversee the Atomic Energy Commission, a government agency in charge of developing atomic science and technology. As part of his job, Gise managed twenty-six thousand people and supervised projects at the Los Alamos laboratory in New Mexico and the Lawrence Livermore laboratory in California.

Gise retired when Bezos was four and bought a ranch in rural Cotulla, Texas. For the next twelve years, Bezos spent every summer on the ranch helping his grandfather with numerous chores. During the long, extremely hot summer days, Bezos fixed windmills, repaired farm equipment, built a barn, and even vaccinated cattle. The ranch was 100 miles (161 km) from the nearest store or hospital, which forced Gise to be self-reliant and resourceful. Jackie recalled her father's inventiveness: "There was

With the help of his grandfather, young Jeff Bezos tinkered with do-it-yourself electric devices on his grandparents' remote farm. He learned to manipulate circuits and solder wires, giving him the confidence to build things on his own.

very little he couldn't do himself. He thought everything was something you could tackle in a garage."[6]

It was in the ranch garage that Bezos learned the science of electronics. At the time, amateur hobbyists could purchase do-it-yourself kits to build stereo amplifiers, ham radios, primitive computers, and other equipment. Gise and Bezos worked together on these projects, tinkering with wires and circuit boards, soldering, and assembling devices. The time spent with his grandfather had a strong influence on Bezos. Lifelong friend Josh Weinstein recalls, "Mr. Gise was a towering figure in Jeff's life."[7]

"Very Nerdy"

Although Bezos loved his grandparents' ranch, he was a kid who looked forward to going back to school in the fall. He valued the learning experience and always worked hard to please his teachers. As he told an interviewer in 2001, "I was a very nerdy and good student. I was in the 'goody goody' class of students and was working hard, studying. I always did my homework on time. I was a good student. I liked school."[8]

Bezos got in trouble only once, and that was due to something beyond his control—and something he is famous for today. Bezos has a crazy-sounding, booming laugh. One time he laughed so loud in class he lost his library privileges—harsh punishment for a nerdy book lover. Bezos said that because of his laugh, his brother and sister were embarrassed to go to the movies with him. His sister complained that at one Disney film, Bezos's laughter drowned out the movie sound track.

When not banned from the library, Bezos spent hours combing the shelves. He loved the fantasy book *The Hobbit* and the Lord of the Rings series by J.R.R. Tolkien. However, he had an equally great passion for science-fiction books by Jules Verne, H.G. Wells, Robert Heinlein, and Isaac Asimov.

Star Trek and Computers

Driven by his love for science fiction, Bezos became a Trekkie, a huge fan of the 1960s science-fiction TV show *Star Trek*. Reruns of the show were aired in Dallas every afternoon at four thirty. Bezos saw each episode so many times he could recite lines of *Star Trek* dialogue along with the actors.

Bezos found a way to pursue his love of *Star Trek* on a primitive computer terminal set up in the hallway of his elementary school. The basic keyboard and tiny video monitor were connected by phone line to a large mainframe computer located in downtown Houston. In this era remote terminals were the only way to reach the Internet, whose use was restricted to government agencies, the military, and universities. For Bezos the terminal was a window into an unexplored digital world.

"I was a very nerdy and good student. I was in the 'goody goody' class of students and was working hard, studying. I always did my homework on time."[8]

—Jeff Bezos, founder of Amazon.

He taught himself how to program the computer. And while using the machine, he discovered a primitive text-based *Star Trek* computer game someone had uploaded. Long before Nintendo and other video games were available to American kids, Jeff and his fellow students spent hours tapping away at the terminal to play the *Star Trek* game.

"Science Fair Central"

Like his grandfather, Bezos spent his time in his own garage working on multiple electronics projects. These were often assembled with parts purchased at Radio Shack electronics stores. When working on a project, he would often ask his mother to drive him to the retailer. As Jackie later recalled, "I think single-handedly we kept many Radio Shacks in business."[9]

"I think single-handedly we kept many Radio Shacks in business."[9]

—Jackie Bezos, Jeff Bezos's mother.

One electronic device was out of reach for Bezos. When he was around twelve, he became obsessed with a battery-operated gadget called the Infinity Cube. It used a set of rotating mirrors to create an optical illusion that the user was staring into an endless tunnel, or "infinity." Bezos could not afford to purchase the Infinity Cube, which cost twenty-two dollars. Unwilling to be denied, he figured out that the pieces of the contraption could be purchased cheaply. After several trips to Radio Shack, Bezos built his own Infinity Cube for a few dollars.

When Bezos was thirteen he created other gadgets, including a solar-powered cooker, a homemade robot, and a crude hovercraft assembled from an old vacuum cleaner. Some of Bezos's projects were created to ensure his privacy, as he later stated: "I was constantly booby-trapping the house with various kinds of alarms and some of them were not just audible sounds, but actually like physical booby-traps. I think I occasionally worried my parents that they were going to open the door one day and have 30 pounds of nails drop on their head or something. Our garage was basically science fair central."[10]

Although Bezos might have frightened his parents, he was difficult to punish. If he did something wrong, he would be grounded and sent to his room. But he was always happy to go because he would simply sit in his room and do what he loved best—work his way through piles of books and magazines.

"The Toughest Lady"

When Bezos was thirteen, his parents began to worry that he was turning into an eccentric bookworm with no friends his age. To help him socialize,

Jackie enrolled Jeff in various youth sports programs. He was terrible at baseball but fared a little better in the Texas youth football league. The slightly built Bezos barely made the league weight limit, and he was not thrilled about playing a game in which much larger boys would tackle him. However, Bezos discovered that his intellect could help him even on the football field. Within two weeks the coach named Bezos the defensive

"It's Harder to Be Kind than Clever"

As a child Jeff Bezos accompanied his grandparents on several vacations. When Bezos gave the commencement speech at Princeton University in 2010, he related an important lesson he learned from his grandfather, Lawrence Preston Gise, during one memorable car trip:

> I was about 10 years old. I was rolling around in the big bench seat in the back of the car. My grandfather was driving. And my grandmother had the passenger seat. She smoked throughout these trips, and I hated the smell. At that age, I'd take any excuse to make estimates and do minor arithmetic. I'd calculate our gas mileage—figure out useless statistics on things like grocery spending. I'd been hearing an ad campaign about smoking. . . . The ad said, every puff of a cigarette takes [two] minutes off of your life. . . .

> I decided to do the math for my grandmother. I estimated the number of cigarettes per day, estimated the number of puffs per cigarette and so on. When I was satisfied that I'd come up with a reasonable number, I poked my head into the front of the car, tapped my grandmother on the shoulder, and proudly proclaimed, "At two minutes per puff, you've taken nine years off your life!". . . My grandmother burst into tears. . . . My grandfather looked at me, and after a bit of silence, he gently and calmly said, "Jeff, one day you'll understand that it's harder to be kind than clever."

Jeff Bezos, "We Are What We Choose," Princeton University, May 30, 2010. www.princeton.edu.

captain. He was the only player on the team who could remember all the plays—and also all the assignments for the other ten boys on his team.

Jeff's football career ended when Mike's job required him to move the family to Pensacola, Florida. After arriving in Pensacola, Jackie wanted to enroll Jeff immediately in the local school's gifted student program. However, the program had a strict one-year waiting period. Jackie showed school officials her son's work and convinced them to disregard the waiting period. Josh Weinstein said, "You want to account for Jeff's success, look at Jackie. She's the toughest lady you'll ever meet and also the sweetest and most loyal."[11]

Two years later the Bezos family moved again, this time to Miami. When Mike Bezos first came to Miami, he was a penniless teenage refugee. Now, sixteen years later, he was an Exxon executive who was able to purchase a large home with a swimming pool in the wealthy Palmetto neighborhood.

Focused on the Future

Ever the good student, Bezos joined the science club and the chess club at Miami Palmetto High School. By this time he had developed a fierce competitive streak and wanted to become class valedictorian. When he announced his goal, all the other smart kids immediately understood they were working for second place. As Weinstein recalled, "He was excruciatingly focused. Not like mad-scientist focused, but he was capable of really focusing, in a crazy way, on certain things. He was extremely disciplined, which is how he is able to do all these things."[12]

Far beyond his high school goals, Bezos focused on outer space. Whereas many kids wanted to be astronauts, Bezos dreamed about becoming a space entrepreneur. He envisioned a tourist business that would ferry visitors to and from the moon. But there was a second reason Bezos wanted to transport humanity to the stars. He worried a giant asteroid might one day crash into earth. If the human race were to be saved, giant orbiting space stations needed to be built. (This idea occurred to Bezos around two decades before the International Space Station was constructed.) To achieve this goal, Bezos focused on amassing a fortune so he could build habitats in space. According to his former high school girlfriend, Ursula Werner, "Jeff always wanted to make a lot of money. It wasn't about money itself. It was about what he was going to do with the money, about changing the future."[13]

"New Ways of Thinking"

Whatever his lofty dreams, Bezos's first summer job, after eleventh grade, was considerably more earthbound. He worked as a fry cook at a local McDonald's restaurant, scrambling eggs, flipping burgers, and working the deep fryer. This experience taught Bezos a valuable lesson; he never wanted to work in a restaurant kitchen again. The following summer Bezos avoided deep-frying by opening his own business. It was a ten-day summer school for fourth-, fifth-, and sixth-graders called the DREAM Institute. DREAM stood for Directed REAsoning Methods, and Bezos was the teacher of these methods.

Jeff Bezos's first summer job was working at a McDonald's restaurant. His unrewarding experience in fast food service convinced him that he needed to create his own opportunities to be happy in the work world.

To drum up business, Bezos printed flyers that he passed out to teachers, students, and parents. For a fee of $600, the DREAM day camp promised to "emphasize the use of new ways of thinking in old areas."[14] Six students eventually signed up for Bezos's DREAM Institute; two of them were his brother and sister.

True to his promise, Bezos covered a diverse array of topics. His students learned about black holes in space, how governments could avoid nuclear war, and how television advertising affected people. Required reading included Robert Heinlein's science-fiction novel *Stranger in a Strange Land* and literary classics like Charles Dickens's *David Copperfield* and Jonathan Swift's *Gulliver's Travels*. Bezos also showed students how to program his family's new Apple II computer.

"Not Smart Enough"

Bezos achieved his high school goal and graduated as valedictorian of his 680-student class. He also won numerous awards. He was one of three members of his class awarded a prestigious academic honor called the Silver Knight Award. Bezos was also honored as best science student for each of his three years in school and was named best math student for two years. Additionally, Bezos won a statewide science fair for an entry about houseflies living in the zero-gravity environment of space.

When Bezos delivered his valedictory speech in 1982, he began with the phrase "space, the final frontier," which is the opening line from the *Star Trek* television show. He spoke earnestly of saving humanity by constructing massive space stations. And he described his dream of turning the earth into a giant nature preserve.

With his top grades and honors, Bezos won early admission to Princeton University. But like many hometown scholars, he discovered his intellect was not that unusual at Princeton. When he entered Princeton in the fall of 1982, he had a goal of becoming a theoretical physicist like his heroes Albert Einstein and Stephen Hawking. Those who practice theoretical physics devise intricate mathematical models to explain complex phenomena like black holes, dark matter, and particle physics.

Although Bezos was one of twenty-five top physics students at Princeton, he struggled to learn the complex theories behind quantum phys-

Jeff Bezos entered Princeton University in 1982 with hopes of becoming a theoretical physicist. However, he was awed by the intellect of other students who excelled at the difficult subject matter that confounded him. Humbled, he made the decision to switch his major to computer science.

ics. Bezos realized he could not compete with the other geniuses in the class. He later recalled:

> There were three or four people in the class whose brains were so clearly wired differently to process these highly abstract concepts, so much more. I was doing well in terms of the grades I was getting, but for me it was laborious, hard work. And, for some of these truly gifted folks—it was awe-inspiring for me to watch them because in a very easy, almost casual way, they could absorb concepts and solve problems that I would work 12 hours on, and it was a wonderful thing to behold. . . . One of the great things Princeton taught me is that I'm not smart enough to be a physicist.[15]

Bezos then made a decision that would change his life—and make him far wealthier than any theoretical physicist. He switched his major to computer science and made a commitment to start his own business.

"Chew on It"

Bezos excelled at computer science in college. By the time he reached his senior year in 1986, he had job offers from major tech companies, including Intel and AT&T. However, Bezos was uninterested in working for a large corporation. He wanted to start his own company but decided he should gain some experience first. He accepted an offer from a tech start-up called Fitel, whose name combined the words *finance* and *telecommunications*. It was cofounded by Graciela Chichilnisky, a professor at Columbia University and the mother of one of Bezos's Princeton classmates. With offices in New York City, London, and Tokyo, Fitel was developing a worldwide network called Equinet. In this era before the Internet, Equinet was designed to link various financial companies engaged in stock trades.

At Fitel, Bezos wrote digital code that allowed stock traders to communicate with one another from computer terminals. The program Bezos developed worked so well that in 1987 he was promoted to associate director of technology and business development. This work required him to travel extensively between New York, London, and Tokyo. According to Chichilnisky, Bezos worked tirelessly and without complaint. "He was not concerned about what other people were thinking," she said. "When you gave him a good solid intellectual issue, he would just chew on it and get it done."[16]

Pasty and Rumpled

In 1988 Fitel was sold to a Japanese company, a change that would have required Bezos to spend more time in Tokyo. This prompted him to take a job with Bankers Trust, a New York financial firm. There Bezos's work involved developing financial software used by the company's pension-fund clients. The software he created was considered revolutionary for the time, and he was promoted to vice president within a year.

Although Bezos was a rising star at Bankers Trust, he felt the company was old-fashioned and stuck in a rut. In his spare time he combed through business magazines and books in search of an unmet need, a problem he could solve by starting his own company. In his studies Bezos researched the lives of successful entrepreneurs and inventors. He was particularly impressed by Alan Kay, a pioneering computer scientist. Kay is best known for developing the graphical user interface, which allows computer users to point and click on screen icons to accomplish various tasks. In a 1984 article in the computer magazine *InfoWorld*, Kay stated, "The best way to predict the future is to invent it."[17] Bezos took this to heart, along with Kay's observation that having a strong vision is worth more than a high IQ.

Bezos worked to develop his point of view by carrying a notebook everywhere he went. When he had a good idea, he would write it down. If a better notion popped into his brain, he quickly scribbled out the old idea. In order to maximize his time working and thinking, Bezos kept a rolled-up

> "The best way to predict the future is to invent it."[17]
>
> —Alan Kay, pioneering computer scientist.

sleeping bag and foam pad in his office in case he did not make it home at night. Business journalist Brad Stone describes the twenty-five-year-old Bezos in this era as "five foot eight inches tall, already balding and with the pasty, rumpled appearance of a committed workaholic."[18]

Working on Wall Street

Bezos was restless and wanted to get out of New York. However, in 1990 an employment recruiter convinced him to join the financial firm D.E. Shaw & Co., or DESCO. Founded by former Columbia University computer science professor David E. Shaw, DESCO was unique on Wall Street because it pioneered the use of computers for stock trading. DESCO used a complex mathematical formula, or algorithm, to compare a stock price in Europe to its counterpart in the United States. If there was a fractional difference between the prices, the software would execute a massive trade, buying low and reselling at a higher price in a matter of seconds. Although a fraction of a cent does not sound like much, multiplied by millions of shares of stock, the formula made DESCO's private investors extremely rich. Today this trading technique is common on Wall Street.

DESCO recruited workers from only the best and brightest mathematicians and computer scientists. But Shaw wanted to expand the company's talent base beyond those with math and computer skills. He believed DESCO would have a better chance of success if the company recruited anyone who graduated at the top of his or her class and who

MacKenzie Bezos

When MacKenzie Tuttle graduated from Princeton University in 1992, her high grades, writing skills, and research work attracted the attention of company recruiters at DESCO, where Jeff Bezos worked. In 1993 Bezos hired MacKenzie and married her six months later. In 2012 MacKenzie Bezos, an author and mother of four, was featured in an article by Rebecca Johnson in *Vogue* magazine:

> Growing up in San Francisco, the daughter of a father who was a financial planner and a mother who cheerfully stayed home to cook meals and decorate the house, MacKenzie was bookish and shy, the kind of girl who would spend hours alone in her bedroom writing elaborate stories. . . .
>
> Bezos acknowledges that having a husband who is worth $20 billion is a stroke of luck—especially for someone who wants to write literary fiction, not the most lucrative profession in the world—but she's also smart enough to know her luck began long before Jeff Bezos showed up in her life. "I am definitely a lottery winner of a certain kind," she says, referring to her husband's success, "and it makes my life wonderful in many ways, but that's not the lottery I feel defined by. The fact that I got wonderful parents who believed in education and never doubted I could be a writer, the fact that I have a spouse I love, those are the things that define me."

Rebecca Johnson, "MacKenzie Bezos: Writer, Mother of Four, and High-Profile Wife," *Vogue*, February 20, 2013. www.vogue.com.

showed extraordinary aptitude in a particular subject. Shaw believed these experts in literature, languages, and others subjects could provide a unique perspective when it came to solving company problems. Bezos would later copy DESCO's hiring practices after he founded Amazon.

"That Fabulous Laugh"

One of the world-class scholars recruited by DESCO was a 1992 Princeton graduate named MacKenzie Tuttle. She was an English major who served as a research assistant for best-selling author Toni Morrison. In 1993 Tuttle was interviewed by Bezos and hired to work for him at DESCO. Although Bezos's wild laugh might have embarrassed his siblings, it did not have the same effect on Tuttle. She explained in a 2012 interview, "My office was next door to his, and all day long I listened to that fabulous laugh. How could you not fall in love with that laugh?"[19]

> "My office was next door to his, and all day long I listened to that fabulous laugh. How could you not fall in love with that laugh?"[19]
>
> —MacKenzie Bezos, Jeff Bezos's wife.

Tuttle decided to win over Bezos by asking him to lunch, and the two fell in love on their first date. Bezos later described Tuttle's attractive qualities in his typical nerdy fashion: "I think my wife is resourceful, smart, brainy, and hot, but I had the good fortune of having seen her résumé before I met her, so I knew exactly what her SATs were."[20] Within three months Bezos and Tuttle were engaged. Three months after that they were married in West Palm Beach, Florida.

At age thirty, Bezos now had a wife and a high-paying, powerful job on Wall Street, but something was still missing. Bezos would not rest until he followed his dream of creating a unique business on the Internet.

Chapter 2

An E-Commerce Pioneer

In 1994 Jeff Bezos was the senior vice president of the Wall Street firm DESCO. His boss, David E. Shaw, put him in charge of finding new business opportunities on the World Wide Web, which had launched in 1991. As he had with every other task going back to high school, Bezos approached his work with a single-minded thoroughness.

While searching through pages of studies, facts, and figures, Bezos discovered that the average web user at the time was a thirty-one-year-old college-educated professional male earning $69,000 a year. Males of this age, income, and education level are known to purchase a wide variety of products. Advertisers call this group a prime demographic.

Bezos made a list of twenty different products that professional men in their thirties might purchase online. (At the time, 82 percent of Internet users were men and 18 percent women.) Of all the products that might be sold, Bezos noticed something special about books. Two giant companies most people had never heard of, the Ingram Book Group and Baker & Taylor, stored and shipped books to most of the country's bookstores.

Ingram and Baker & Taylor were the mainstays of the book businesses. Most independent bookstores at the time kept fewer than twenty-five thousand titles on their shelves. Large bookstores might have five or six times that number. When a customer wanted a book that was not on the shelf, the store would order the title from one of the two distributors. Bezos discovered something else: the distributors maintained an electronic list called Books in Print that contained the titles of 3 million books that were available from publishers at that time. Most of the books were stored on wooden pallets in the distributors' warehouses.

Bezos viewed the electronic version of Books in Print as a gold mine. He realized he could act as a middleman, selling books online by purchasing them from the distributors. Books in Print would allow him to sell any book to any person anywhere in the world. As he stated in 2008:

> I was . . . looking for something that you could only do on the Web. And having a bookstore with universal selection is only possible on the Web. You could never do it with a paper catalogue. The paper catalogue would be the size of dozens of New York City phone books, and it would be out of date the second you printed it. You know, the largest book superstores carry about 150,000 titles, and there aren't very many that big.[21]

No Regrets

Bezos wanted DESCO to start an online book business, so he presented his conclusions to Shaw. He said one figure stuck in his head: the Internet was growing by an astounding 2,300 percent a year. Shaw did not think the book business was a good fit for his Wall Street company. Bezos offered his resignation. He later recalled his thinking at the time, "When I'm 80 am I going to regret leaving Wall Street? No. Will I regret missing a chance to be there at the beginning of the Internet? Yes."[22]

Bezos had a dream, but the idea of profiting from the book business seemed crazy in the early 1990s. Although the Internet was growing rapidly, no one knew whether people would buy products online. Additionally, most of the independent bookstores located in the United States were struggling financially. As editor and publisher Steve Wasserman explains, "Bookselling in the United States had always been less of a business than a calling. Profit margins were notoriously thin, and most independent stores depended on low rents. Walk-in traffic was often sporadic, the public's taste fickle; reliance on a steady stream of bestsellers . . . was not exactly a sure-fire strategy for remaining solvent."[23]

> "Having a bookstore with universal selection is only possible on the Web. You could never do it with a paper catalogue."[21]
>
> —Jeff Bezos, founder of Amazon.

Many bookstores were struggling financially when Jeff Bezos made the decision to open an online marketplace for books. Still, he believed an online store could offer customers more choices than brick-and-mortar establishments and therefore gain an edge in the industry.

Despite the hazards associated with the book business, Americans spent about $19 billion on books in 1994. This translated into sales of 513 million individual books, which included seventeen best sellers that sold more than 1 million copies each.

Moving to Seattle

After Jeff Bezos quit his job, he went home and told his wife, MacKenzie, about his unique idea for selling books over the Internet. He said he wanted to move from New York to Seattle to start a company. MacKenzie had no qualms. "I have no business sense whatsoever," she recalled, "but I saw how excited he was."[24] Soon they were piloting a Chevrolet Blazer across the country to Seattle. As MacKenzie drove, Jeff wrote up a thirty-page Amazon business plan on a manual typewriter.

Jeff Bezos chose Seattle for several reasons. The world headquarters of Microsoft was in nearby Redmond, which attracted skilled tech workers to the region. The University of Washington, located in Seattle, had a world-class computer science school. And the Roseburg, Oregon, warehouse of Ingram Book Group was a six-hour drive from Seattle.

Bezos also choose Seattle for financial reasons. In 1992 the Supreme Court ruled that retailers do not have to charge sales tax in states where they do not have a physical presence. Bezos originally wanted to locate his business in California, which had a population of 30 million. However, if he had done so, he would have had to collect sales tax from this large number of people. By locating his business in Washington, which had a population of 4.8 million at the time, Bezos only had to charge sales tax to a much smaller number of potential in-state customers.

By avoiding sales tax collection in other states, Bezos could undercut prices charged by brick-and-mortar bookstores, which were required to collect taxes in states where they were located. As Wasserman writes, Bezos "would use this advantage to avoid collecting hundreds of millions of dollars in state sales taxes, giving Amazon an enormous edge over retailers."[25]

Relentless.com

On July 5, 1994, Bezos incorporated his company as Cadabra, Inc., a name taken from *abracadabra*, the word often uttered by stage magicians when performing a trick. However, Bezos's lawyer pointed out that people tended to hear *Cadabra* as *cadaver*, the word for "corpse." After renting a home in the Seattle suburb of Bellevue, Bezos and his wife held brainstorming sessions to devise a better name. During this period they registered various Internet domain addresses, or URLs, that they might possibly use, including Awake.com, Browse.com, and Bookmall.com. One of their favorites, Relentless.com, summed up Bezos's personality when it came to business. Friends thought the relentless URL sounded too sinister. However, anyone typing Relentless.com into a web browser to this day will be taken to the Amazon website.

In October Bezos finally picked a name. He wanted something that began with the letter *A* so it would come up near the top of any alphabetical listing. While searching the *A* section of the dictionary, he came across Amazon, the earth's largest river. Since he envisioned founding the earth's largest bookstore, the name stuck. He registered the web address on November 1, 1994.

"Pretty Iffy"

While working out a company name, Bezos hired his first employee, Shel Kaphan, a computer programmer from Santa Cruz, California. Kaphan

Jeff Bezos appears quite at home, laughing while perched on a table at an Amazon office. In 1999, when this photo was taken, Amazon's headquarters were located in Seattle's beautiful Pacific Tower, a far cry from the cramped Bezos family garage where the company began operations.

was recommended to Bezos by a programmer at DESCO. The Amazon office was set up in the Bezos's garage, a damp, chilly workspace heated with an old-fashioned woodstove. Bezos backed Amazon with $300,000 of his own money. Kaphan was paid $64,000 annually, half of his previous salary. His contract required him to contribute $5,000 to Amazon.

With a relatively small budget for a start-up, Bezos did not want to spend money on fancy office furniture. He built two desks out of wooden doors purchased for sixty dollars each at a local lumber store. According to Kaphan, "The whole thing seemed pretty iffy at that stage. There wasn't really anything except for a guy with a barking laugh building desks out of doors in his converted garage. . . . I was taking a big risk by moving [to Seattle] and accepting a low salary."[26]

Bezos's parents, Mike and Jackie, had no doubts about Amazon. In early 1995 they invested $100,000 in the company, most of their savings. Mike read Jeff's business plan and did not even know what the Internet was. However, as Mike later stated, "As corny as it sounds, we were betting on Jeff."[27] For his part, Jeff warned his parents that Amazon had a 70 percent chance of failure. But he still wanted to be able to come home at Thanksgiving if things did not work out.

> "The whole thing seemed pretty iffy at that stage. There wasn't really anything [to the Amazon company] except for a guy with a barking laugh building desks out of doors in his converted garage."[26]
>
> —Shel Kaphan, Amazon's first employee.

Blowing Fuses

MacKenzie Bezos worked as Amazon's first accountant, writing checks and handling financial matters. Soon the company hired another employee, Paul Davis, a British programmer. Davis had previously been on staff at the University of Washington's computer science and engineering department. When he left this secure job, Davis's coworkers were so sure he was making a huge mistake that they jokingly took up a collection for him. They passed around an empty coffee can and raised a few dollars in case he needed to buy food in the future.

Davis might have questioned his decision to join Amazon when he began setting up the company's network computers. The machines drew so much power that they continually blew fuses in the garage. To solve the problem, Jeff ran long orange extension cords to other electrical outlets in the house. These, too, would blow fuses if MacKenzie used her hair drier.

Jeff Bezos had to worry for only a few months about keeping the lights on at Amazon. In the spring of 1995, Bezos moved the company into a small office above a tile store near downtown Seattle. The company converted the small basement in the building into a warehouse. The room had previously been a band practice studio, and the words "Sonic Jungle" were painted on the black door. Leaving the suburbs behind, Jeff and MacKenzie moved into a small apartment nearby.

"Welcome to Amazon.com Books!"

Once the Amazon beta website was online in the spring of 1995, Bezos and Kaphan sent out links to family, friends, and colleagues. The first Amazon site was quite primitive, meant to work with the slow Internet telephone modems of the era. The headline proclaimed, "Welcome to Amazon.com Books!" The link below read, "One million titles, consistently low prices."[28] The original company logo was a simple blue box with an illustrated letter *A* inside. A graphic of a river wound through the letter.

Kaphan sent an Amazon link to his friend John Wainwright. On April 3, 1995, Wainwright became Amazon's first customer, purchasing a science book called *Fluid Concepts and Creative Analogies*. In 2008, Wainwright was honored by Bezos for being his first customer. When Amazon built its new South Lake Union headquarters in Seattle, one of the buildings was named "Wainwright."

Helping Customers

Despite its somewhat amateurish look, the Amazon site contained several unique features that are now seen on nearly every website. Amazon offered a virtual shopping basket and a secure way to enter credit card numbers into a web browser. The search engine was able to hunt through millions of entries taken from the Books in Print database. Users could search by title, author, subject, or a unique identifier called the International Standard Book Number, or ISBN.

Hiring "the Best and Brightest"

Jeff Bezos only wanted to hire what he called "high-IQ brainiacs" to work at Amazon. Business journalist Brad Stone explains Bezos's hiring practices:

Bezos felt that hiring only the best and brightest was key to Amazon's success. For years he interviewed all potential hires himself and asked them for their SAT scores. "Every time we hire someone, he or she should raise the bar for the next hire, so that the overall talent pool is always improving," he said. . . . That approach caused plenty of friction. As Amazon grew, it badly needed additional manpower, and early employees eagerly recommended their friends, many of whom were as accomplished as they were. Bezos interrogated the applicants, lobbing the kind of improbable questions that were once asked [by his previous employer] D. E. Shaw, like "How many gas stations are in the United States?" It was a test to measure the quality of a candidate's thinking; Bezos wasn't looking for the correct answer, only for the individual to demonstrate creativity by coming up with a sound way to derive a possible solution. And if the potential employees made the mistake of talking about wanting a harmonious balance between work and home life, Bezos rejected them.

Brad Stone, *The Everything Store: Jeff Bezos and the Age of Amazon.* New York: Little, Brown, 2013, pp. 43–44.

Another unique feature, the customer book review section, was designed by Kaphan, who also wrote the first review. It was about a book called *Bitter Winds: A Memoir of My Years in China's Gulag*. Kaphan read the book cover to cover after finding it on a shelf in the Amazon warehouse, where it was awaiting shipment to an early customer. Other Amazon customer reviews were written by friends, family, and employees. Bezos believed the reviews were extremely important. He thought that Amazon would generate customer loyalty by helping people decide whether or not they wanted to buy a book.

Naturally, some reviews were negative, which created controversy. One book publisher wrote Bezos an angry letter explaining that bookstores were supposed to sell books, not criticize them. Bezos did not agree, stating, "We saw it very differently. When I read that letter, I thought, we don't make money when we sell things. We make money when we help customers make purchase decisions."[29] Bezos also believed that customer reviews created a way for the online community to interact as if they were meeting one another in bookstores.

Bezos added other features that were aimed at reassuring customers that Amazon was a legitimate, safe way to purchase books. The company sent an instant e-mail confirmation for each order and offered a liberal thirty-day return policy.

"It's Not My Mom"

Amazon opened its site to the public on July 16, 1995. One of the company engineers devised a way for a bell to ring every time a customer placed an order. To everyone's surprise, the bell starting dinging almost immediately and continued to ring. At first Bezos asked the employees in the room, "Is that your mom? It's not my mom. I don't recognize this person. Is that a friend of yours?"[30] Bezos later said the experience was one of the most emotional of his life.

After a few days the bell had to be disconnected because it was ringing nonstop. Without any advertising, Amazon processed more than $12,400 worth of orders the first week. Within a month Amazon had shipped books to all fifty states and forty-five foreign countries. Perhaps it is not surprising that many of the early orders were related to computers and the Internet. One best seller was called *How to Set Up and Maintain a World Wide Web Site*.

With Amazon's early success, Bezos proved that the Internet was a modern new way to buy books. However, the company's shipping practices were stuck in the nineteenth century. When a customer purchased a book on the website, Amazon simply phoned in an order for the title

Amazon's first shipping center was run by a handful of employees packing boxes in a low-ceilinged basement of a rented building in Seattle. Today, the company has huge, well-staffed warehouses (pictured) situated in cities all over the world.

from Ingram or Baker & Taylor. When the book arrived in the mail several days later, Amazon repackaged it and shipped it to the customer. Most books arrived at a customer's doorstep within a week; rare titles could take up to a month.

As business grew, Amazon took over the entire basement of its rented building. However, shipping orders was a grueling task. Amazon had ten employees who programmed computers all day. At night they went to the low-ceilinged basement to pack books until three or four o'clock in the morning. The work was not only tiring, it was physically painful. And although Bezos was an Internet wizard, he was somewhat oblivious when it came to making this job easier. As he later recalled:

> When we started out, we were packing on our hands and knees on these cement floors. One of the software engineers that I was packing next to was saying, You know, this is really killing my knees and my back. And I said to this person, I just had a great idea. We should get kneepads. And he looked at me like I was from Mars. And he said, Jeff, we should get packing tables. We got packing tables the next day, and it doubled our productivity.[31]

The knee-pad story has been repeated many times by Jeff, MacKenzie, and early Amazon employees. It is among company lore known as "Jeffisms," stories that sum up Bezos's unique or nerdy way of thinking.

Losing Money Fast

Even with the addition of packing tables, Amazon could not keep up with the orders that were pouring in over the Internet. Two months after the website launched, the company was selling around $20,000 worth of books a week. But only about half of the weekly orders were being fulfilled, while the rest were piling up in a major backlog. And the company had no personnel to handle returns, which were also stacking up due to Amazon's generous returns policy.

Although there were many day-to-day issues, Amazon's biggest problem was that it was not making money. Distributors sold books for 50 percent off the price printed on the cover, or the list price. Amazon offered most books for 40 percent off the list price, which meant it was making only 10 percent profit, or one dollar on a ten-dollar book.

In order to keep Amazon's doors open, Bezos spoke to investors in hopes of raising $1 million. But he did not have much to offer. The company lost $52,000 in 1994 and was set to lose $300,000 in 1995. However, Bezos had grand ambitions and predicted the company would be bringing in anywhere from $74 million to $114 million annually by 2000. (Amazon succeeded far beyond Bezos's most optimistic predictions. In 2000 the company sold $1.64 billion worth of merchandise.)

The Everything Store

Beyond the numbers, Bezos informed investors that Amazon would totally change the world of online commerce. He said customers would flock to the site because it offered convenience over large, crowded bookstores. With its reviews and book recommendations, Amazon offered what Bezos saw as a personalized shopping experience unlike any other on the Internet. Bezos also predicted something that others did not foresee at the time. He said one day everyone would be using high-speed Internet connections far faster than the telephone modems of the day. Bezos describe a future in which Amazon would offer a near-infinite selection of merchandise. He sold the concept by calling Amazon "The Everything Store."

Bezos was a smooth talker and very persuasive. As one of Amazon's first investors, Eric Dillon, recalled, "He swept me off my feet. He was so convinced that what he was doing was basically the work of God and that somehow the money would materialize. The real wild card was, could he really run a business? That wasn't a gimme. Of course, about two years later I was going, 'Holy ****, did we back the right horse!'"[32]

Dillon was among fifteen investors who believed in Bezos; many others turned him down. However, by November 1995 Bezos had raised $980,000. By early 1996 Amazon was rated as a $10 million company by respected financial analysts.

> "He swept me off my feet. He was so convinced that what he was doing was basically the work of God and that somehow the money would materialize."[32]
>
> —Eric Dillon, an early Amazon investor.

Training Goldfish

Bezos realized that Amazon could be a multibillion dollar company, and he was not alone. In May 1996 the influential *Wall Street Journal* gave the company a big boost by running a front-page story on Amazon. The article was so positive it could have been written by Bezos himself, and the day after it ran, Amazon orders doubled.

Amazon soon moved into a 17,000-square-foot (1,580 sq. m) building. The new office was filled with desks assembled from wood doors, furniture that had become part of the company's tradition. Bezos lived

"Changing Consumers' Lives"

In May 1996 the *Wall Street Journal* ran an extremely positive front-page story about Amazon under the headline "Wall Street Whiz Finds Niche Selling Books on the Internet." Journalist G. Bruce Knecht wrote that few book publishers even knew of Amazon's existence and that the company's website was an "underground sensation" for book lovers who spend hours searching its vast catalog and reading its often amusing customer reviews. Knecht describes Amazon's unique appeal:

> Amazon has caught fire because, unlike most retailers, Mr. Bezos has found a way to use the Web's technology to offer services that a traditional store or catalog can't match. An Amazon customer can romp through a database of 1.1 million titles (five times the largest superstore's inventory), searching by subject or name. When you select a book, Amazon is programmed to flash other related titles you may also want to buy. If you tell Amazon about favorite authors and topics, it will send you by electronic mail a constant stream of recommendations. You want to know when a book comes out in paperback? Amazon will e-mail that too.
>
> Although a relatively small company, Amazon provides a singular case in which the frequently hyped Web is actually changing consumers' lives. It also suggests how on-line retailing could change the way publishers market books. "Amazon is the beginning of a completely new way to buy books," says Alberto Vitale, chairman of book-publishing giant Random House Inc. "It could increase book sales quite dramatically by making it easier for people to find the books they want."

G. Bruce Knecht, "Wall Street Whiz Finds Niche Selling Books on the Internet," *Wall Street Journal*, May 16, 1996. www.wsj.com.

near the new headquarters but kept a sleeping bag in his office for all-night work sessions. Amazon grew to include thirty-three employees. Three were gifted book editors who wrote book reviews and picked featured books. This was meant to give Amazon a strong literary voice similar to that of a trusted independent bookseller. Amazon hired others to upgrade computer systems and pack books. Whatever their job descriptions, Bezos hired only employees considered to be the best and the brightest, or as he defined them, "people who had been successful in everything they had done."[33]

Amazon continued to focus on its customers, which could now be found in sixty-six countries. To keep things interesting, Bezos kept an online list of the most obscure or humorous titles ordered. He felt this provided a snapshot of the diversity, behavior, and interests of Amazon customers. Some of Bezos's favorite titles included *Training Goldfish Using Dolphin Training Techniques*, *How to Start Your Own Country*, and *Sponging: A Guide to Living Off Those You Love*.

Get Big Fast

Because of its then unique business practices, about 60 percent of Amazon's orders came from repeat customers. And Bezos envisioned expanding that customer base to suit everyone's needs. When one employee said he was a kayak enthusiast, Bezos told him that one day Amazon would sell more than books about kayaks. It would also sell subscriptions to kayak magazines, tickets for kayak travel tours, and even kayaks, paddles, life jackets, and other kayaking equipment. The employee thought Bezos sounded a little bit crazy but did not underestimate him.

At the end of 1996, Amazon had not yet celebrated its second anniversary, but the company was growing beyond even Bezos's expectations. However, as sales approached $16 million, Amazon had yet to make a profit. In fact, Amazon was expected to lose around $6 million. Bezos spent everything that came in, and borrowed more, to build better computer networks and hire more employees.

Despite the losses, investors were betting on Bezos to be a success. At the beginning of 1997, Amazon's value had increased to $60 million. Bezos could have sold the company and retired at age thirty-three. But obtaining money was not his main goal. Bezos's vision was summed up by a new Jeffism that became Amazon's motto: Get Big Fast.

Chapter 3

Earth's Largest Bookstore

In early 1997 Jeff Bezos was frantic. The total number of Internet users had reached 70 million, and Bezos was anxious to sell books to every one of them. The more books Amazon sold, the faster the company could grow and the more ground it could occupy on the Internet. Although Amazon was already the number one online bookseller, Bezos pressed his employees to improve shipping times and make the company's website easier to use.

> "When you are small, someone else that is bigger can always come along and take away what you have."[34]
>
> —Jeff Bezos, founder of Amazon.

To keep Amazon growing, Bezos and many of the company's 150 workers commonly arrived at six o'clock in the morning. Some stayed to work past midnight. No one took a day off during the week unless they were very ill, and many worked through the weekends to live up to Bezos's motto to get big fast. When asked why he was so obsessed about rapid expansion, Bezos answered, "When you are small, someone else that is bigger can always come along and take away what you have."[34]

The Barnes & Noble Threat

When it came to someone taking away what Amazon had, Bezos thought of Barnes & Noble. At the time Barnes & Noble was the biggest bookstore in America, with about $2 billion in annual sales. In the early 1990s the company began a huge expansion, building book superstores in malls across the country. This played a large role in wiping out small independent bookstores. Between 1991 and 1997, as Barnes & Noble grew, the number of independently owned book shops fell from forty-five hundred to around three thousand. And the slide seemed likely to continue.

Amazon's sales amounted to a small fraction of Barnes & Noble's, but the CEO of Barnes & Noble, Len Riggio, was making plans to destroy Amazon. Riggio told Bezos that Barnes & Noble was going to launch its own website. He suggested that Bezos consider selling Amazon to Barnes & Noble to save himself the public humiliation of being crushed by the larger company. But Bezos believed that as a unique company dedicated to its customers, Amazon would triumph.

Bezos turned down Riggio's offer. This prompted Internet analyst George Colony to write that after Barnes & Noble launched its website, Bezos would have to change his company's name to "Amazon.Toast."[35] To ease his worries, Bezos began taunting Barnes & Noble with mischievous

In the late 1990s huge chain bookstores like Barnes & Noble had cornered the market in the United States. Barnes & Noble even hoped to crush Amazon by opening its own webstore. Jeff Bezos, however, predicted Amazon's unique customer service model would prevail over the competition.

stunts. Amazon held boisterous business meetings with potential investors in the café of the Seattle Barnes & Noble. And he hired trucks with mobile billboards to drive by Barnes & Noble stores with the words "Can't find that book you wanted?"[36] along with the Amazon logo and website address.

Warehouses and Workers

Bezos had another major problem with Barnes & Noble and other bookstores in general. Buyers who wanted best sellers could buy them in a bookstore and not wait a week or more to receive the book in the mail. To address this issue, Amazon began to stock around two hundred thousand top-selling books in a massive 93,000-square-foot (8,640 sq. m) warehouse near Seattle's famed Pike Place Market. Amazon also opened a warehouse in Delaware. With its two new facilities, Amazon could offer same-day shipping for around 95 percent of its orders.

As Amazon grew, Bezos went on a hiring spree, pilfering executives from established companies like FedEx, his old employer DESCO, and even Barnes & Noble. Bezos also hired David Risher, a top executive who worked nearby at Microsoft. When Risher told his boss, Microsoft founder Bill Gates, he was leaving to go work for Amazon, Gates was astounded. Gates underestimated the power of the Internet at that time and thought Amazon was destined to fail.

Bezos hired Joy Covey as Amazon's chief financial officer. She went to work on a plan to raise a large sum of money through what is called an initial public offering, or IPO. With an IPO, a privately owned company "goes public," offering millions of shares of stock for a certain price. If investors believe the company will be profitable, the price can climb on the first day the shares are offered. In such cases the company offering the IPO can collect hundreds of millions of dollars in a single day. Bezos believed an IPO would raise Amazon's public profile and solidify its reputation as a cutting-edge tech company.

A Federal Lawsuit

Bezos was taking a great risk when he went forward with the IPO. Amazon was not even two years old, and the company had never turned a

To Our Shareholders

After Jeff Bezos took Amazon public in 1997, he wrote a letter telling shareholders exactly what he planned to do in the coming years. The letter, excerpted below, is now considered a classic business playbook, read by those hoping to build successful companies:

- We will continue to focus relentlessly on our customers.

- We will continue to make investment decisions in light of long-term market leadership considerations rather than short-term profitability considerations or short-term Wall Street reactions....

- We will continue to learn from both our successes and our failures.

- We will make bold rather than timid investment decisions where we see a sufficient probability of gaining market leadership advantages. Some of these investments will pay off, others will not, and we will have learned another valuable lesson in either case....

- We will work hard to spend wisely and maintain our lean culture. We understand the importance of continually reinforcing a cost-conscious culture, particularly in a business incurring net losses.

- We will balance our focus on growth with emphasis on long-term profitability. . . . At this stage, we choose to prioritize growth because we believe that scale is central to achieving the potential of our business model.

- We will continue to focus on hiring and retaining versatile and talented employees. . . . We know our success will be largely affected by our ability to attract and retain a motivated employee base, each of whom must think like, and therefore must actually be, an owner.

Jeff Bezos, "To Our Shareholders," Business Insider, November 16, 2011. www.businessinsider.com.

profit. As Bezos and Covey traveled the United States and Europe to speak to wealthy investors, they faced questions about profitability. They were also asked why Amazon did not sell other products in addition to books. Many investors were skeptical and told Bezos that Barnes & Noble was going to annihilate Amazon.

Bezos's problems multiplied on May 12, 1997. Only three days before the planned IPO, Barnes & Noble finally unveiled its new website. The same day, Barnes & Noble filed a lawsuit against Amazon in federal court. The suit accused Amazon of false advertising because it billed itself as the earth's largest bookstore. According to a statement in the lawsuit, "[Amazon] isn't a bookstore at all. It's a book broker."[37] The Barnes & Noble lawsuit was later settled out of court. The terms were not disclosed, but Amazon continued to claim it was the world's largest bookstore.

> "This is Day 1 for the Internet and, if we execute well, for Amazon.com."[39]
>
> —Jeff Bezos, founder of Amazon.

"An Internet Star"

Despite the attempt by Barnes & Noble to sink Amazon, the IPO on May 15 was a huge success. Amazon stock was initially offered on the NASDAQ stock exchange for $18 per share. By the end of the day, the price climbed to more than $23, allowing Amazon to raise $54 million in a single day. The company was now valued at $429 million. Tech journalist Richard L. Brandt explains why investors were willing to back the IPO: "Amazon had become the premier Internet commerce site. With a two-year head start over the competition, huge brand-name recognition, and growth in revenues, it had become an Internet star."[38]

On the day of the stock offering, Bezos called Amazon's offices from New York. He urged employees, some of whom owned thousands of stock shares, not to focus on the price. Instead, they should keep serving Amazon customers. The Seattle employees bought a few cases of inexpensive beer, passed bottles around the offices, and went back to work. However, the Amazon IPO made many people rich, including Bezos and his parents, who were now multimillionaires.

At the end of 1997, Bezos sent a letter to Amazon shareholders that noted the company's revenue had grown by 838 percent that year. Bezos also stated that things were just getting started:

This is Day 1 for the Internet and, if we execute well, for Amazon.com. Today, online commerce saves customers money and precious time. Tomorrow, through personalization, online commerce will accelerate the very process of discovery. Amazon.com uses the Internet to create real value for its customers and, by doing so, hopes to create an enduring franchise, even in established and large markets.[39]

The letter was very unusual for the way it addressed its investors. Rather than promising quick riches, Bezos vowed that Amazon would make decisions based on long-term growth rather than short-term profits. And

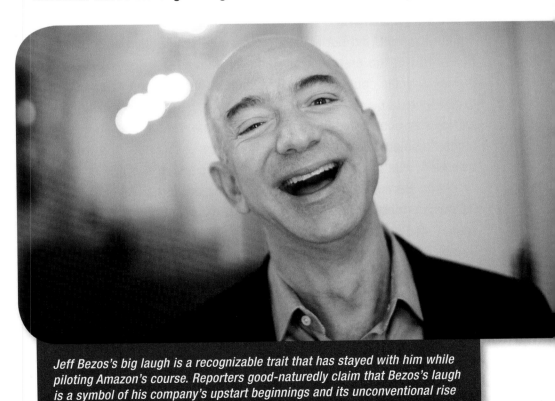

Jeff Bezos's big laugh is a recognizable trait that has stayed with him while piloting Amazon's course. Reporters good-naturedly claim that Bezos's laugh is a symbol of his company's upstart beginnings and its unconventional rise to success.

he listed hurdles to growth, including well-funded competition. Despite the letter's cautious tone, investors were not discouraged. In fact, it helped increase the value of Amazon stock. By 1998 the stock was selling for $105 per share and the company was valued at $5 billion. By mid-January 1999 Bezos's net worth had climbed to over $9 billion.

With his wealth and success, Bezos became a media superstar whose face was featured on dozens of magazines, newspapers, and websites. Nearly every article mentioned Bezos's laugh, which was said to symbolize Amazon. Bezos laughed as his company rose from nothing, ignored the traditional rules of marketing, and became the biggest and most disruptive force on the Internet. However, Bezos's laugh conveyed more than humor; he laughed when he was happy, frustrated, or sad. As Bezos stated, sometimes he laughed "because I'd be crying otherwise."[40]

A Move to Music

The Amazon IPO did not end the company's competition with Barnes & Noble. But in the end Amazon came out ahead. As Bezos anticipated, Barnes & Noble could not compete online. The company was structured to distribute large numbers of books to a relatively small number of brick-and-mortar bookstores. When Barnes & Noble tried to shift its business model to shipping single books to thousands of customers, it was overwhelmed, which resulted in numerous delays and errors.

While Barnes & Noble foundered, Amazon surged ahead. This led business writers to begin using a new term. "Getting Amazoned"[41] became a code phrase for what could happen to old-style businesses like Barnes & Noble that failed to adapt to the new rules of the Internet.

Whatever the fortunes of Barnes & Noble online, Amazon had its own problem. It was revealed in a 1998 survey conducted by a company executive. The survey showed that the large majority of consumers would never use the Amazon website because most Americans never bought a book. Bezos did not seem troubled by America's poor reading habits; he got excited and viewed the problem as a challenge to be overcome.

Bezos formed what he called a SWAT team, composed of recently hired Harvard Business School graduates. The team conducted a search for products like books that were easy to ship through the mail but could not be fully stocked on retailer's shelves. The team concluded there were hundreds of thousands of music and video titles and only a fraction were available in stores. (This was during an era when music and video streaming was uncommon due to slow Internet connections.)

Earth's Biggest Selection

After the SWAT team conducted its research, Bezos decided first to sell music CDs on Amazon and offer movies later in the year. In June 1998 the motto on top of Amazon's website changed from "Earth's Largest Bookstore" to "Books, Music, and More." Soon after, it changed again to "Earth's Biggest Selection." Consumers could now scroll through 125,000 CD titles, about ten times more than those offered by brick-and-mortar music stores. As it had with books, Amazon offered the CDs at a steep discount and featured customer reviews and preference-based recommendations. In addition, Amazon offered a new and exciting feature; customers could listen to short audio clips of each song before purchasing an album.

"The way you become a leader [in online retail] is to focus obsessively on the customer experience."[42]

—Jeff Bezos, founder of Amazon.

Investors were skeptical of Bezos's move into the music business. There was already a successful company, CDNow, that had been selling music online since 1994. The *Wall Street Journal* called Bezos's move risky. The paper stated in an editorial that Amazon was diluting its reputation as a home for its loyal, book-loving customers. Bezos answered his critics as he always had, by focusing on customers: "Online commerce is a big arena. It's not going to be the case where you have one company who dominates this marketplace. You are going to have a leader, and clearly, we want to be that leader in every area that we enter. And the way you become a leader is to focus obsessively on the customer experience."[42] Once again Bezos triumphed over those who underestimated him. Amazon sold $14 million worth of CDs in four months, far outstripping sales of CDNow. (In 2001 Amazon bought CDNow and eventually merged the company with its own operations.)

Visitors to Amazon could now buy music and books with extremely little effort, thanks to a new feature called 1-Click Shopping. Customers who stored their credit card information, shipping addresses, and preferences on Amazon's computers could simply select the 1-Click Shopping button on the web page to make a purchase and confirm their order. The idea for 1-Click Shopping originated with Bezos, who correctly assumed that Amazon could make additional millions by reducing the time customers had to spend between browsing for goods and buying a product.

A Bezos Shopping Spree

In November 1998 Amazon began selling videocassettes and DVDs of movies and TV shows on its website. By the end of the year, Amazon was the largest seller of movies on the Internet. With more products to sell, Bezos needed to build more warehouses and hire more people. To do so he was quickly able to raise an additional $1.25 billion from eager investors assured by the company's success.

Despite the massive cash infusion, Bezos was notoriously stingy. He made employees pay for parking at the downtown warehouse and required executives to fly coach rather than first class. However, Bezos was not so stingy when he went on a dot-com buying spree. Bezos spent millions buying the Internet Movie Database (IMDb), which featured detailed information and reviews about films, television shows, and computer games. Amazon also bought a few European competitors, the British online bookstore BookPages and the German site Telebuch. These were relaunched as Amazon.co.uk and Amazon.co.de respectively.

In order sell a wider variety of products, Bezos founded a pharmacy website called Drugstore.com. He invested in numerous existing online retail specialists, including Pets.com, Wineshopper.com, and Homegrocer .com. Bezos also snapped up websites that seemed to point to a new way of doing business online. He purchased a site called Junglee for $170 million. Started by three Stanford graduates, Junglee offered shoppers price comparisons for goods sold by various online companies. Bezos wanted to incorporate Junglee's listings into the Amazon site so customers could find any imaginable product even if it was not offered by Amazon. However, some company executives disliked Junglee because it directed customers away from Amazon to make purchases elsewhere. As a result, Junglee never received support from Amazon executives, and the rejection resulted in the company's failure at the end of 1999.

Toys for Tots

Bezos wanted to expand Amazon's distribution system by tenfold. In 1999 the company spent $300 million to build new distribution centers and retrofit old ones in the United States. The company also opened several new warehouses in Europe. Bezos, who had built robots in his garage as a kid, equipped the distribution centers with the latest automated technology. Blinking lights on aisles and shelves guided workers to products that were placed on conveyor belts. The belts were connected to giant machines called Crisplants that scanned, sorted, and provided customer addresses for each item.

With its rapid growth, Amazon began offering an expanded list of products on its website in 1999. Consumers could purchase electronics, software, games, sporting goods, and even greeting cards. However, Amazon ran into trouble when it wanted to sell toys. Unlike books, which are distributed by two large companies, toys are sold by hundreds of different manufacturers. To sell toys, Amazon would have to buy them in bulk from each company, rather than order them as needed. And whereas unsold books could be returned to publishers, unsold toys were not returnable.

Bezos saw a challenge and decided to spend $120 million filling Amazon warehouses with everything from Barbie dolls and *Star Wars* action figures to cheap plastic sand pails and wooden train sets. Amazon executives predicted disaster, but Bezos wanted toys. He even said he would drive the unsold stock to the landfill himself, until someone pointed out that he drove a Honda Accord, which would require many trips.

When the Christmas shopping season arrived, Amazon customers eagerly snapped up toys online. The company was so overwhelmed with orders that Seattle tech employees were sent off to work in distribution centers around the country and housed frugally in motels, two to a room. Despite Amazon's best efforts to fill all orders by Christmas, many customers were left without gifts. And the company was left with about half of the toys it purchased. This led Bezos to make a huge contribution of unsold merchandise to the Toys for Tots charity after the holidays.

"The King of Cyber-Commerce"

Whatever the problems, Amazon's 1999 sales were up by 95 percent over the previous year. The company now boasted 3 million new customers, bringing the total of registered accounts to 20 million. And the number of Amazon employees had exploded from fifteen hundred in 1998 to seventy-six hundred at the end of 1999.

Time magazine took note of Amazon's growth and named Bezos the Person of the Year. At age thirty-five Bezos was the fourth-youngest person to ever hold that honor. *Time* called Bezos "the king of cyber-commerce [who] helped build the foundation of our future."[43] *Time's*

1999
Jeff Bezos

FOR THEIR LAST SELECTION of the 20th century, TIME'S editors chose the man whose entrepreneurial vision promised to help shape the ... pioneer Jeff Bezos. The founder

In 1999, Time *magazine named Jeff Bezos its Person of the Year. Time's managing editor, Walter Isaacson, noted that Bezos best represented the dot-com boom that saw the rapid investment in and expansion of Internet industries and the resulting meteoric rise of online shopping.*

managing editor, Walter Isaacson, said that naming the Person of the Year is usually a difficult task, but it was easy in 1999 "because there were two great themes of the year—online shopping and 'dot-com' mania. The minute we thought of Bezos, it was obvious that he embodied both."[44] Bezos later said that the honor *Time* bestowed on him made his mother so happy she cried.

"Amazon.bomb"

Being named Person of the Year was only one positive occurrence in Jeff Bezos's life. MacKenzie was pregnant for the first time, and the couple had recently purchased a $10 million mansion on the shores of Seattle's Lake Washington.

Amazon was also celebrating an incredible year. A study showed that 42 percent of all online shoppers chose Amazon during the holiday season. And in the few years since its founding, Amazon had become a household name recognized by more than half of all Americans. In 2000 Bezos rolled out a new logo; the word *Amazon* with an arrow that curved from the *A* to the *z*. The new logo, which also suggested a smile, symbolized that any product from A to Z could be found on Amazon's website.

Despite the positive news, Amazon was burning through money at an alarming rate. In 1999 the company lost $720 million and ended the year $2 billion in debt. Engineer Gene Pope commented, "What we are doing here is building a giant rocket ship, and we're going to light the fuse. Then it's either going to go to the moon or leave a giant smoking crater in the ground."[45] The financial journal *Barron's* picked up on Pope's smoking crater imagery and took to calling the company "Amazon.bomb."[46]

The Dot-Com Bomb

Questions about Amazon's future were heightened when the NASDAQ stock market index began to yo-yo. For years stock prices of tech and Internet companies, including Amazon, had been on a steady upward trend. Investors had been supremely confident about new technology

> "There were two great themes of [1999]—online shopping and 'dot-com' mania. The minute we thought of Bezos, it was obvious that he embodied both."[44]
>
> —Walter Isaacson, managing editor of *Time*.

A Company Built on a Bubble

In 1999 *New York Times* reporter Peter de Jonge visited an Amazon distribution center in Seattle at a time when questions about the company's future were making headlines. In the article, excerpted below, de Jonge describes the work situation for Amazon employees:

> Despite the ample accomplishments and serious, unresolved challenges, it is the peculiar fate of Amazon.com that both are completely overshadowed by the sensational valuation and volatility of its stock. For all its all-nighters and tattooed punks humping books in the distribution center and golden retrievers wandering the halls in the corporate office, Amazon.com is a $20 billion, 2,100-employee company built on the thin membrane of a bubble, and this brings a manic [instability] to the place that no amount of profitless growth can diminish.
>
> Working at Amazon right now . . . seems designed to deny the enormous distraction of the looming [stock] ticker and to somehow maintain the confidence that the fate of the company still lies wholly in its own hands. . . . [Employees] are beseeched not to concern themselves with the stock price, to keep their heads down and to continue focusing obsessively on satisfying the needs of their customers. But there is a slightly hysterical quality to these exhortations.

Peter de Jonge, "Riding the Wild, Perilous Waters of Amazon.com," *New York Times*, March 14, 1999. http://partners.nytimes.com.

and the future. Although many tech companies were losing money, there was a widespread belief that most Internet businesses would someday be profitable. This created what was called the dot-com bubble, in which stock prices inflated like a giant soap bubble. The bubble was at its largest on March 10, 2000, when the NASDAQ index reached an all-time high of 5,048.

All bubbles pop, and after the NASDAQ peak, investors began to see that online companies were not living up to expectations. There was a massive sell-off of stocks, creating what is now called the dot-com bust. The stock price of hundreds of tech and online companies collapsed. Companies like Pets.com disappeared completely, while others lost a large portion of their value, which forced them to downsize and lay off workers. Amazon's value also plunged; by the end of 2000 Amazon stock, which was selling for $106 per share at the end of 1999, was trading for $15.

The collapse of Amazon stock created stress for the company's employees. Through it all, Bezos remained strangely calm. Amazon senior vice president Mark Britto recalled the contrast in attitudes between employees and the boss: "We were all running around the halls with our hair on fire thinking, *What are we going to do?* [But not Jeff.] I have never seen anyone so calm in the eye of a storm. Ice water runs through his veins."[47]

Perhaps Bezos was unruffled because he was sure that Amazon was turning a corner. Instead of getting big fast, he was now focused on cutting costs and shutting down unprofitable aspects of the online business. And Bezos probably let go with one of his famous laughs when he saw Amazon's financial reports. Despite the low stock prices and frazzled employees, Amazon was due to make a profit in 2001.

> "[We're] building a giant rocket ship, and we're going to light the fuse. Then it's either going to go to the moon or leave a giant smoking crater in the ground."[45]
>
> —Amazon engineer Gene Pope.

Chapter 4

Taking Risks

In January 2002 Jeff Bezos finally had some good news for investors. Amazon had earned its first profit—$5 million on sales of more than $1 billion. Although the number was modest, Amazon's stock price immediately rose more than 40 percent. The profit boosted investor confidence in Bezos, who was searching for new methods for Amazon to make money with its state-of-the-art technology. Over the years, Bezos had hired the world's best computer scientists to build one of the most advanced digital networks on earth.

By the early twenty-first century, this massive network of computer servers, websites, and distribution processing systems was considered 99.9 percent reliable. This meant computer crashes and errors were practically nonexistent. The amazing reliability of Amazon's network was attractive to competitors such as Target, Toys "R" Us, Circuit City, and Borders. All had experienced website crashes and shipping errors when rolling out their online businesses. To solve their problems, the corporations decided to partner with Bezos, trading use of Amazon's computer network for investment money or discounted inventory.

Amazon's network also served as the foundation for Amazon Web Services (AWS). Created in 2002, AWS offers what is known as cloud computing. For a fee, AWS clients can run their websites on the company's servers. As tech writer Mark Harris explains, "The idea behind cloud computing is deceptively simple. Instead of buying and maintaining your own computing hardware, why not simply rent hard drive space, database storage and computing power from a company such as Amazon? Let them worry about operating systems, security patches and upgrades, while you get on with running your business—and saving money."[48] Bezos took the

amazon
web services

AWS Products & Solutions ▾

Tier

applications, test existing
applications in the cloud, or simply gain

Launched in 2002, Amazon Web Services offers storage and software options that companies can purchase and use remotely. With their computing operations hosted on Amazon servers, these companies no longer need to invest in expensive computer hardware to do business.

profits from AWS and went on a building binge, creating giant computer data centers around the globe.

Prime Crazy

In 2005 Bezos generated more money with Amazon Prime. For an annual fee of seventy-nine dollars, subscribers would receive free two-day shipping on 1 million items available from Amazon. (The price of Prime was raised to ninety-nine dollars in 2014.) As usual, skeptics questioned Bezos's logic, focusing on two concerns. Either the seventy-nine-dollar sign-up fee would be too expensive or, conversely, too many would sign up for Prime, causing Amazon to lose money on shipping. According to Greg

Greeley, vice president of Amazon Prime Global, "Skeptics thought we were crazy then. We built up a delivery service—that meant one thing to individuals. But then we added [Amazon Prime] and people thought we were a bit nuts. . . . [But] we never thought it wasn't going to work. This was one

The Bezos Family Foundation

In 2000 Mike and Jackie Bezos, as well as Jeff's siblings (but not Jeff), founded the Bezos Family Foundation with the fortune they made from their Amazon investments. The Bezos family has long been interested in gifted-student programs; Jeff participated in several such programs while growing up. Perhaps it is no surprise, then, that the Bezos Family Foundation invests in innovative student-driven learning programs that depart from conventional classroom experiences. New York City school administrator Paul Perry describes the foundation's educational investments:

> [The Bezos Family Foundation] has been ramping up its giving, from $3.4 million in 2010 to $15 million in 2012. . . . [Its] investments have fallen into three main categories: Early Learning, Excellence in K–12 Education, and Youth Leadership and Engagement. The Early Learning work pushes the use of the latest neuroscience research to improve early learning environments . . . pushing the integration of recent advancements in brain science into the curriculum and [teaching practices] of pre-school programs. . . .
>
> The youth engagement and leadership work is a longstanding passion of Mike and Jackie Bezos, and the Bezos Scholars Program, which aims to empower high school juniors and their teachers, is a signature effort now [in] its tenth year. The program promotes student-led projects to expand learning outside of the classroom and . . . trains student leaders and provides them with resources to solve local issues in their communities. . . . The Bezos Family Foundation is making it clear that they believe in the power of students to take the lead and learn.

Paul Perry, "The Bezos Family Foundation Is All About Education. Here's What They're Doing," Inside Philanthropy, 2014. www.insidephilanthropy.com.

experiment we knew we were going to make work—failure was not an option."[49] Bezos was not worried about failure; he did not think of Amazon Prime as a shipping program but as a convenience program that would make fast shipping an everyday experience. As he predicted, the service was popular; tens of thousands of customers signed up for Amazon Prime on the first day it was launched.

In 2011 Prime added Amazon Instant Video to its offerings. This service provided Prime subscribers access to around five thousand movies and TV shows. In 2014 the service expanded to include Prime Music, giving members unlimited access to more than 1 million songs. Although Amazon has long refused to release figures concerning Prime, estimates by consumer research groups indicate that the service had around 40 million members in 2015.

> "We never thought [Amazon Prime] wasn't going to work. This was one experiment we knew we were going to make work—failure was not an option."[49]
>
> —Greg Greeley, vice president of Amazon Prime Global.

Kindling Interest in Books

In 2007 Bezos challenged skeptics once again when Amazon introduced a $359 e-book reader called Kindle. During the previous decade several companies, including electronics giant Sony, had produced e-readers. All had failed to catch on with the public. But Kindle was different. Whereas other e-readers resembled primitive tablet computers, Kindle did not have a backlit screen. It used a black-and-white screen Bezos described as "electronic ink"[50] to mimic paper.

Weighing little more than 10 ounces (283 g), Kindle was lighter than a paperback and could hold about two hundred books. And it was not necessary to connect Kindle to a personal computer to obtain books. Users with Wi-Fi connections could shop with the device and download books directly from Amazon. The device could also be used to read newspapers and magazines.

In 2009 Bezos announced the launch of Kindle 2, an upgraded model. The new e-reader was slimmer and offered more memory than the previous version and included a text-to-speech option that read text aloud.

When Bezos launched Kindle 2, he said, "Our vision is every book, ever printed, in any language, all available [from Amazon] in less than 60 seconds."[51] However, only about twenty thousand books were digitized at that time. Bezos feared Kindle would die unless consumers could purchase a large number of e-books. Using Amazon's power as the world's largest bookseller, Bezos pushed publishers to convert one hundred thousand published books into e-books.

While the publishers complied, Bezos created controversy by insisting that all e-books be sold for $9.99. There was no particular reason he picked that price, other than people expected e-books to cost less than hardcover best sellers, which sold for around $28 at the time. However, publishers demanded that Amazon pay $12 wholesale for each e-book. Amazon complied but then sold the book at a loss, for $9.99. This started a book war pitting Bezos against what were called the Big Six publishers—Hachette, HarperCollins, Macmillan, Penguin, Simon & Schuster, and Random House.

> "Our vision is every book, ever printed, in any language, all available [from Amazon] in less than 60 seconds."[51]
>
> —Jeff Bezos, founder of Amazon.

The publishers raised their wholesale prices to pressure Bezos to raise his prices, but he refused. Then publishers started to delay the release of e-books for up to seven months after the hardcover books went on sale. Bezos still refused to change his pricing practices. He also retaliated against some publishers who refused his terms, removing their books from Amazon's website. Without access to Amazon, a publisher's sales could plunge by 50 percent.

iPad Versus Amazon

In 2010 the battle between Amazon and book publishers took a new turn after Apple released the first-generation iPad to widespread acclaim. The iPad was not only useful for reading e-books, but it was also a fully functioning tablet computer that cost only ten dollars more than the Kindle 2. The iPad was instantly popular, and it provided a new marketplace for e-books. Five of the Big Six publishers signed deals with Apple to sell e-books on the iTunes Store. With the agreement, publishers could set their own prices for the books, and Apple took a 30 percent commission on each title sold.

Bezos had long viewed the iTunes Store as a major threat. Apple first opened the store in 2003 to sell downloadable songs for ninety-nine cents each. In the next few years, Apple became the number one music merchant in the United States, quickly bypassing Amazon, Best Buy, and Walmart. The songs on iTunes were compatible with the extremely popular iPod music player. Bezos now feared the iPad, with its iBooks app, would lead to a major downturn in what remained Amazon's main business, selling books.

The threat from Apple was heightened when Macmillan began selling books on the iTunes Store. In addition, Macmillan told Bezos that it would continue not making its best sellers available to Amazon for seven months after the hardcover was published if he continued to sell its e-books for $9.99. Bezos reacted with a controversial move; Amazon deleted the "Add to Cart" button from all Macmillan titles on its website. This outraged customers, publishers, and reviewers. A few days later Amazon returned the shopping cart button and gave in to the demands of the publishers. Bezos agreed to raise e-book prices to $13.99. However, the iPad was so popular that Apple was soon able to claim 20 percent of the e-book market, selling titles for $12.99 to $14.99.

Kindle Direct Publishing

Bezos had another way of going after publishers who interfered with his business methods. For more than a century, large publishing houses based in New York City decided which authors to support, what books would be published, and how much authors would be paid. After his quarrel with Macmillan, Bezos moved to make it easier for writers to completely bypass the publishing industry. Bezos created Kindle Direct Publishing so writers could self-publish their books in the Kindle format. Writers could use Kindle Direct for free and receive up to 70 percent of purchase price when the books sold on Amazon. Authors who wished to sell printed books could use another Amazon service, CreateSpace, which published books only after they were ordered.

Kindle Direct Publishing received a huge boost in 2010 when news stories described the success of twenty-six-year-old Amanda Hocking, a paranormal romance writer from Minnesota. Hocking made $2 million on

Amazon selling nine hundred thousand e-books about vampires in love. Others, such as science-fiction writer Hugh Howey and mystery-thriller writer J.A. Konrath, have successfully self-published with the service.

Taking on Tablets

As much as Bezos disliked Apple, Amazon was forced to recognize the popularity of the company's products. In 2010 Amazon reluctantly released a Kindle app for Macintosh so e-books could be read on iPhones, iPads, and Apple computers. Bezos also wanted an Amazon version of the iPad. This resulted in the launch of the Kindle Fire, a tablet computer, in 2011. The original Kindle Fire sold for $199, about $300 less than the second-generation iPad 2. The Fire cost about $180 to produce, but Bezos planned to make money selling digital content for the computer, including books, music, and videos.

Within a year, about 7 million Fires were purchased, making it the second-best-selling tablet after the iPad 2. In 2013 Amazon introduced the Fire HDX in two screen sizes, the HDX 7 and the HDX 8.9. Priced at $397, the HDX 8.9 was $100 cheaper than the new iPad Air, but Kindle sales slumped. In 2013 Fire dropped to number four in tablet sales, lagging behind offerings from Apple, Samsung, and ASUS.

The Smartphone Fail

Whatever the sales figure, the Kindle Fire was highly rated by tech reviewers. The same could not be said for what was perhaps Bezos's biggest blunder. In June 2014 Amazon unveiled the Fire Phone, a smartphone with a starting price of $199 (with a two-year service contract). The Fire Phone had the same features as similarly priced smartphones such as Android models and the iPhone.

The Fire Phone had several features that set it apart, including 3-D graphics. The phone also had a unique system called Firefly that identified text, sounds, and scanned objects. Once a book, piece of music, or item was recognized, Firefly took users to the Amazon website where it could be purchased. Amazon blogger David Isbitski explains, "Firefly understands your surroundings, instantly helping you to learn more, discover new things, and take action on the world around you. It can scan physical objects, identify them, and obtain related information about them. Everything from book covers, album covers, bar codes, QR codes, movies, television shows, songs and more."[52]

The Kindle Fire is Amazon's answer to the popular Apple iPad. Launched in 2011, the Fire plays music and videos and can run the Kindle digital reader application. Jeff Bezos set the price well below that of his competition, hoping to gain ground in the market and later make up costs in the sale of digital content.

Although two-thirds of smartphones sold in 2014 were produced by Apple and Samsung, Bezos did not need to sell a lot of Fire Phones to make money. Firefly was designed to make it easier for customers to order from Amazon. The Fire Phone even had a physical "Buy" button on the side that allowed users to purchase an item on the phone's screen when pressed. As tech analyst Ramon Llamas explains: "I don't think they're in this to say, 'Hey, we want you [to] make phone calls and do social media.' They want to sell you stuff. That's been Amazon's mission since day one. And what's changed since then is the world has gone much more mobile than before."[53]

Amazon's mission failed to impress the public. With the Fire Phone coming seven years after the first iPhone and six years after Android phones, Amazon needed something that was breathtaking. Instead, reviewers called the Fire Phone clunky, forgettable, mediocre, and a shopping machine. By the end of 2014, Amazon was selling the phone for ninety-nine cents. Amazon was left with $83 million worth of unsold Fire Phones, and the company announced that it lost $170 million on costs related to the device.

> "I don't think [Amazon was making smartphones] to say, 'Hey, we want you [to] make phone calls and do social media.' They want to sell you stuff."[53]
>
> —Ramon Llamas, tech analyst.

The Netflix Challenge

The Fire Phone was one of two risky ventures pushed by Bezos. While taking on Apple and Android, Amazon was also moving to compete with Netflix. Netflix had long been known for its DVD-by-mail and on-demand Internet media streaming. However, in 2013 Netflix attracted attention for its high-quality television series *House of Cards* and *Orange Is the New Black*. Both shows won raves from critics and numerous awards. With a wish to challenge Netflix, Bezos founded Amazon Studios and invested $100 million to produce original content.

In 2013 Amazon Studios produced its first series, *Alpha House*, a political satire starring John Goodman and written by *Doonesbury* cartoonist Garry Trudeau. The series failed to attract much attention. However, critics called Amazon's next offering, the dark comedy *Transparent*, the best new show of 2014 regardless of network or platform. Later in the year *Transparent* won several Golden Globe Awards, beating *Orange Is the New Black* in the comedy category.

Hoping to continue its run of rave reviews, Amazon signed several veteran filmmakers to create original shows. They included Ridley Scott, known for his science-fiction blockbusters, and Alex Gibney, a documentary filmmaker. In 2015 Amazon made a deal with comedy filmmaker Woody Allen to produce a show. Although the seventy-nine-year-old Allen continued to tap out scripts on a manual typewriter, he said he was excited to produce a series for the digital era.

Betting on Old Media

Even as Amazon moved into the production of new media, Bezos shocked the business world with his purchase of an old-media institution. In late 2013 Bezos paid $250 million to purchase the *Washington Post*, one of the nation's oldest newspapers. When the deal was announced, it was made clear that Bezos was buying the paper in a personal capacity; it would not become one of Amazon's numerous subsidiaries.

The *Washington Post* is famous for exposing the Watergate scandal that led to the resignation of President Richard Nixon in 1974. The story of the two *Washington Post* reporters who investigated the scandal, Bob Woodward and Carl Bernstein, was turned into the award-winning film *All the President's Men*.

Like the book business, the news industry experienced major changes with the growth of the Internet. As more people came to rely on websites for their news, newspapers struggled financially. The *Washington Post* is a good example of this trend. In 1993 the paper had around 1,000 reporters and a daily circulation of 832,000. By early 2013 the number of reporters had dropped to around 640 while circulation bottomed out at 474,000. The paper was in such dire financial straits that the owners considered selling the iconic headquarters where the paper has been published since 1950.

When Bezos purchased the *Washington Post*, there was optimism that he could revive the paper. As newspaper consultant Alan D. Mutter stated, "I believe [Bezos] bought the newspaper because he wants to re-envision the enterprise and The Post is an iconic world brand. He knows something about building iconic world brands."[54]

Bezos said very little to the press when he bought the *Post*, but in 2014 he admitted that he was originally skeptical about investing in an old-media industry. However, after purchasing the paper, Bezos followed his usual business strategy; he invested a large sum of money in hopes of reaping profits in the future. The *Post* hired around one hundred new employees to create blogs and other digital media. With its updated website, the *Post* began attracting millions of new visitors. In June 2014, 39 million people visited the *Post* website, up 63 percent from the previous year.

> "[Bezos] bought the newspaper because he wants to re-envision the enterprise and The Post is an iconic world brand. He knows something about building iconic world brands."[54]
>
> —Alan D. Mutter, newspaper consultant.

Drone Delivery

When Bezos bought the *Washington Post*, some critics joked that the paper would someday be delivered by drones. They were referring to Bezos's 2013 proposal called Prime Air. When Amazon customers used Prime Air, their packages would be delivered by drones within thirty minutes.

In Amazon's early days Bezos took packages full of books to the post office every night in a Chevrolet Blazer. But small unmanned aircraft systems, or drones, have long fascinated the robot-loving Bezos, who once built a hovercraft in his garage. And Bezos was excited when he discussed the Prime Air drone tests, which were conducted in a large, cage-like test area. "I saw the 10th or 11th generation of the drone, flying around in the cage, and it's truly remarkable," Bezos said. "It's not just the physical airframe, electric motors, and so on—the most interesting part of this is the autopilot, the guidance and control, the machine vision systems that make it all work."[55]

According to Bezos, 86 percent of Amazon packages weigh less than 5 pounds (2.3 kg). They could easily be delivered by drones, which travel at speeds of 50 miles per hour (80 kph). However, the commercial use of drones is strictly regulated by the Federal Aviation Administration (FAA), a government agency that oversees all aspects of civil aviation.

Because the majority of packages shipped by Amazon weigh less than five pounds, Jeff Bezos looked at the possibility of utilizing aerial drones to take over delivery duties. Amazon began testing the drones for this purpose, but government restrictions on commercial flight have hindered progress.

The FAA put in place numerous rules that stopped the rollout of Prime Air. According to the FAA, commercial drone operators have to be certified pilots of manned aircraft. Drones can fly only during the day, must remain below 400 feet (122 m), and must remain in view of the operator. Bezos hired numerous lawyers and lobbyists to petition Congress and the FAA to change the rules on drone delivery. Due to various safety concerns, it remains unclear if Prime Air will ever launch.

Four Hundred Twenty-Six Items per Second

Drone delivery is not the only risky futuristic concept put forth by Bezos. In 2003 he opened an aerospace company called Blue Origin in a massive

Seattle warehouse. Bezos hopes to use Blue Origin to advance his dream of space tourism, but little else is known about the secretive company. In 2014 Bezos did reveal a few details about Blue Origin; the company was investing in a program to build rocket engines.

Whatever the future of space travel, Amazon's business continued to soar. By 2014 the company Bezos started with a few programmers in his garage employed 117,000 people. An average of 162 million people visited Amazon every month, and the company had revenues of more than $74 billion. During the run-up to the 2014 Christmas season, Amazon was selling 426 items per second, or 27,720 per minute. And Bezos's net worth topped $33 billion.

Amazon's growth, however, did not come without controversy. Amazon's low prices are blamed for driving major brick-and-mortar stores into bankruptcy, including Circuit City and Borders. Bezos's battles with

Blue Origin

Jeff Bezos has long dreamed of building space hotels, amusement parks, and orbiting space colonies to house up to 3 million people. To follow that dream, Bezos founded the aerospace company Blue Origin in 2003. Two years later Bezos bought a massive tract of Texas land the size of Rhode Island to build a Blue Origin rocket-testing ground and spaceport.

Little happened with the company, and Bezos rarely mentioned it until 2011, when he launched a website for Blue Origin with the statement: "We're working to lower the cost of spaceflight so that many people can afford to go and so that we humans can better continue exploring the solar system. Accomplishing this mission will take time, and we're working on it methodically." Bezos's plans included developing a rocket that would have capabilities for vertical takeoff and vertical landing. In 2014 Bezos invested $500 million of his own money in Blue Origin with the goal of launching a test rocket by 2019.

Quoted in Leonard David, "Amazon.com's Jeff Bezos Relaunches Secretive Private Spaceship Website," Space.com, November 18, 2011. www.space.com.

publishers added to his large number of detractors. And Bezos has been blamed for not contributing much to charity even as his mother and father gave away millions made from their Amazon investment.

Perhaps the strongest criticism aimed at Bezos is that Amazon has rarely been a profitable enterprise; Bezos spends money as fast as Amazon makes it in his desire to grow at any cost. If it were an old-fashioned, low-tech retailer, Amazon would likely have declared bankruptcy long ago.

Whatever the charges against Bezos, he seems to have been born with ambition, a willingness to take risks, and a desire to act as a disruptive force in the marketplace. He knew exactly what he wanted to do while driving across the country to Seattle in 1994, and he seems to know exactly what he wants to do more than two decades later. From books to cloud computing, from TV shows to drones, Bezos has defied expectations and worked tirelessly to create the biggest store on earth.

Introduction: A Better Way of Doing Things

1. Quoted in Richard L. Brandt, *One Click: Jeff Bezos and the Rise of Amazon.com*. New York: Penguin, 2011, p. 36.

2. Quoted in Brad Stone, *The Everything Store: Jeff Bezos and the Age of Amazon*. New York: Little, Brown, 2013, p. 12.

3. Jeff Bezos, "We Are What We Choose," Princeton University, May 30, 2010. www.princeton.edu.

Chapter One: Resourceful and Intelligent

4. Quoted in Stone, *The Everything Store*, p. 5.

5. Michael Granberry, "Jeff Bezos; at Amazon.com, He's the Mouth That Roared," *Dallas Morning News*, August 8, 1999. www.dallasnews .com.

6. Quoted in Stone, *The Everything Store*, p. 147.

7. Quoted in Chip Bayers, "The Inner Bezos," *Wired*, July 2002. http:// archive.wired.com.

8. Quoted in Academy of Achievement, "Interview: Jeff Bezos," November 26, 2013. www.achievement.org.

9. Quoted in Bayers, "The Inner Bezos."

10. Quoted in Academy of Achievement, "Interview."

11. Quoted in Stone, *The Everything Store*, p. 149.

12. Quoted in Stone, *The Everything Store*, p. 150.

13. Quoted in Luisa Yanez, "Jeff Bezos: A Rocket Launched from Miami's Palmetto High," *Miami Herald*, August 5, 2013. www.palmettohigh alumni.org.

14. Quoted in Bayers, "The Inner Bezos."

15. Quoted in Academy of Achievement, "Interview."

16. Quoted in Stone, *The Everything Store*, pp. 19–20.

17. Quoted in Jim Bartimo, "Smalltalk with Alan Kay," *InfoWorld*, June 11, 1984, p. 62.

18. Stone, *The Everything Store*, p. 21.

19. Quoted in Rebecca Johnson, "MacKenzie Bezos: Writer, Mother of Four, and High-Profile Wife," *Vogue*, February 20, 2013. www.vogue.com.

20. Quoted in Johnson, "MacKenzie Bezos."

Chapter Two: An E-Commerce Pioneer

21. Quoted in Keenan Mayo and Peter Newcomb, "How the Web Was Won," *Vanity Fair*, July 2008. www.vanityfair.com.

22. Quoted in "Everything You Need to Know About Jeff Bezos," *Daily Beast*, August 5, 2013. www.thedailybeast.com.

23. Steve Wasserman, "The Amazon Effect," *Nation*, May 29, 2012. www.thenation.com.

24. Quoted in Johnson, "MacKenzie Bezos."

25. Wasserman, "The Amazon Effect."

26. Quoted in Stone, *The Everything Store*, p. 33.

27. Quoted in Stone, *The Everything Store*, p. 33.

28. Quoted in Belle Beth Cooper, "The First Version of Google, Facebook, and YouTube and More," *BufferSocial* (blog), February 13, 2014. https://blog.bufferapp.com.

29. Quoted in Adi Ignatius, "Jeff Bezos on Leading for the Long-Term at Amazon," *Harvard Business Review*, January 3, 2013. https://hbr.org.

30. Quoted in Mark Leibovich, *The New Imperialists*. Paramus, NJ: Prentice Hall, 2002, p. 89.

31. Quoted in Mayo and Newcomb, "How the Web Was Won," *Vanity Fair*.

32. Quoted in Stone, *The Everything Store*, p. 42.

33. Quoted in Kieran Levis, "Amazon," Kieranlevis.com, 2010. www.kieran levis.com.

Chapter Three: Earth's Largest Bookstore

34. Quoted in Stone, *The Everything Store*, p. 52.

35. Quoted in Leibovich, *The New Imperialists*, p. 90.

36. Quoted in Leibovich, *The New Imperialists*, p. 90.

37. Quoted in Reference for Business, "Amazon.com," 2015. www.refer enceforbusiness.com.

38. Brandt, *One Click*, p. 96.

39. Jeff Bezos, "To Our Shareholders," Business Insider, November 16, 2011. www.businessinsider.com.

40. Quoted in Leibovich, *The New Imperialists*, p. 93.

41. Quoted in Leibovich, *The New Imperialists*, p. 93.

42. Quoted in Brandt, *One Click*, p. 111.

43. Quoted in Associated Press, "Amazon.com Founder Is *Time*'s Person of the Year," *Los Angeles Times*, December 20, 1999. http://articles .latimes.com.

44. Quoted in Associated Press, "Amazon.com Founder Is *Time*'s Person of the Year."

45. Quoted in Stone, *The Everything Store*, p. 72.

46. Jacqueline Doherty, "Amazon.bomb," *Barron's,* May 31, 1999, http:// online.barrons.com.

47. Quoted in Stone, *The Everything Store*, p. 102.

Chapter Four: Taking Risks

48. Mark Harris, "You Can Fire Us on a Minute's Notice," *Guardian* (London), March 25, 2009. www.theguardian.com.

49. Quoted in Hayley Tsukayama, "What Amazon's Learned from a Decade of Prime," *The Switch* (blog), *Washington Post*, February 2, 2015. www.washingtonpost.com.

50. Quoted in Caroline McCarthy, "Amazon Debuts Kindle E-Book Reader," CNET, November 19, 2007. www.cnet.com.

51. Quoted in Brad Stone and Motoko Rich, "Amazon in Big Push for New Kindle Model," *New York Times*, February 9, 2009. www.nytimes.com.

52. David Isbitski, "Announcing the Amazon Fire Phone: App and Game Experiences Never Before Possible," Amazon, June 18, 2014. www .amazon.com.

53. Quoted in Timothy Stenovec and Dino Grandoni, "Amazon Announces a 3D Phone called 'Fire Phone,'" *Huffington Post*, June 18, 2014. www.huffingtonpost.com.

54. Quoted in Christine Haughney, "Bezos, Amazon's Founder, to Buy the *Washington Post*," *New York Times*, August 5, 2013. www.nytimes .com.

55. Quoted in Jillian D'Onfro, "Jeff Bezos Says Amazon's Delivery Drones Are 'Truly Remarkable,' but You Probably Won't See Them Soon," Business Insider, December 2, 2014. www.businessinsider.com.

Important Events in the Life of Jeff Bezos

1964

Jeffrey Preston Bezos is born on January 12 in Albuquerque, New Mexico.

1977

Bezos learns to program computers at age thirteen.

1982

Bezos attends Princeton University.

1988

Bezos takes a job at Bankers Trust, where he develops financial software.

1990

Bezos joins the New York financial firm D.E. Shaw & Co., or DESCO, where he quickly advances to become senior vice president.

1993

Bezos marries MacKenzie Tuttle after a six-month courtship.

1994

Bezos quits DESCO to start an online bookstore. On July 5 he incorporates his new company as Cadabra, Inc., and changes the name to Amazon in October.

1995

The Amazon website goes live on July 16.

1996

Amazon is valued at $10 million by Wall Street analysts.

1997

Amazon's initial public offering on Wall Street raises more than $54 million, and the company is valued at $429 million.

1998

As Amazon continues to grow, the company's value rises to more than $5 billion.

1999

Amazon introduces 1-Click Shopping to simplify the purchasing process.

2000

The dot-com bubble bursts, and Amazon is one of the most high-profile losers as its stock tumbles from a high of $106 to $15 a share.

2001

Amazon earns its first profit, $5 million on $1 billion in sales.

2003

Apple opens the online iTunes Store, resulting in a major drop in Amazon's music sales.

2005

Bezos creates Amazon Prime, offering subscribers free two-day shipping on 1 million items.

2007

Amazon introduces the Kindle e-book reader.

2010

Amazon launches Kindle Direct Publishing, a service that allows authors to self-publish their books in the Kindle format and sell them online.

2011

Amazon introduces the Kindle Fire, a tablet computer.

2013

Amazon Studios produces its first television series, *Alpha House*.

2014

Amazon begins selling the Fire Phone, a smartphone that is panned by critics and ignored by the public.

For Further Research

Books

Corinne Grinapol, *Reed Hastings and Netflix*. New York: Rosen Classroom, 2013.

Jessie Hartland, *Steve Jobs: Insanely Great*. New York: Schwartz & Wade, 2015.

Aurelia Jackson, *Amazon®: How Jeff Bezos Built the World's Largest On-line Store*. Broomall, PA: Mason Crest, 2014.

Angie Smibert, *12 Great Moments That Changed Internet History*. Seattle: Amazon Digital Services, 2014. Kindle edition.

Erika Wittekind, *Amazon.com*. Minneapolis: ABDO, 2013.

Websites

Amazon (www.amazon.com). One of the world's most popular retail websites, with links to Amazon Web Service, Prime, IMDb, and more than 200 million products.

Bezos Expeditions (www.bezosexpeditions.com). A website that lists more than twenty-five different Bezos personal and philanthropic investments, including the 10,000 Clock, the Seattle Museum of History & Industry, and the Center for Neural Circuit Dynamics.

Bezos Family Foundation (www.bezosfamilyfoundation.org). The Bezos Family Foundation was founded by Jeff Bezos's parents, Mike and Jackie Bezos, and his siblings. This site provides details about millions of dollars the foundation has provided for educational programs throughout the world.

Blue Origin (www.blueorigin.com). Jeff Bezos launched this website in 2011 for his secretive space-tourism company, Blue Origin. The site details

Bezos's plans for developing rockets and taking spaceflights with the goal of establishing colonies in space.

Jeff Bezos, TED (www.ted.com/speakers/jeff_bezos). This site features two popular TED Talks by Jeff Bezos, including the 2010 Princeton University graduation address in which the Amazon founder makes the case that character is reflected by the choices people make over the course of a lifetime.

Index

Picture Credits

About the Author

Stuart A. Kallen is the author of more than three hundred nonfiction books for children and young adults. He has written on topics ranging from the theory of relativity to the art of animation. In addition, Kallen has written award-winning children's videos and television scripts. In his spare time, he is a singer/songwriter/guitarist in San Diego.